First Facts®
Map Mania

Are We There Yet?

Using Map Scales

by Doreen Gonzales

Consultant: Susanna A. McMaster, PhD
Associate Director, MGIS Program
Geography Department, University of Minnesota

Hi! I'm Ace McCaw. Map scales really measure up! And anyone can use them. Come on, I'll show you.

Capstone

Mankato, Minnesota

First Facts is published by Capstone Press
151 Good Counsel Drive, P.O. Box 669, Mankato, Minnesota 56002
www.capstonepress.com

Library of Congress Cataloging-in-Publication Data
Gonzales, Doreen.
 Are we there yet? : using map scales / by Doreen Gonzales.
 p. cm. —(First facts. Map mania)
 Summary: "Describes what map scales are and how to use them to compare map
distances to real distances"—Provided by publisher.
 Includes bibliographical references and index.
 ISBN-13: 978-1-4296-0053-8 (hardcover)
 ISBN-10: 1-4296-0053-5 (hardcover)
 1. Map scales—Juvenile literature. I. Title.
GA118.G66 2008
912.01'48—dc22   2006100038

Editorial Credits
Jennifer Besel, editor; Bobbi J. Wyss, Veronica Bianchini, and Linda Clavel, designers;
 Bob Lentz, illustrator; Wanda Winch, photo researcher

Photo and Map Credits
AP Photo, 20
Blue Earth County Environmental Services, 9 (photo)
Capstone Press/Karon Dubke, cover, 10 (photos of maps), 21
Corbis/London Aerial Photo Library, 14
Google Maps Imagery/NAVTEQ data (c) Google Inc. and NAVTEQ. Used with permission,
 10 (maps)
Maps.com, 4–5, 6–7, 8, 9, 10–11, 12–13, 15, 16–17, 18–19 (maps)
NASA/GSFC/LaRC/JPL, SRTM/MISR Teams, 8 (photo)

1 2 3 4 5 6 12 11 10 09 08 07

Table of Contents

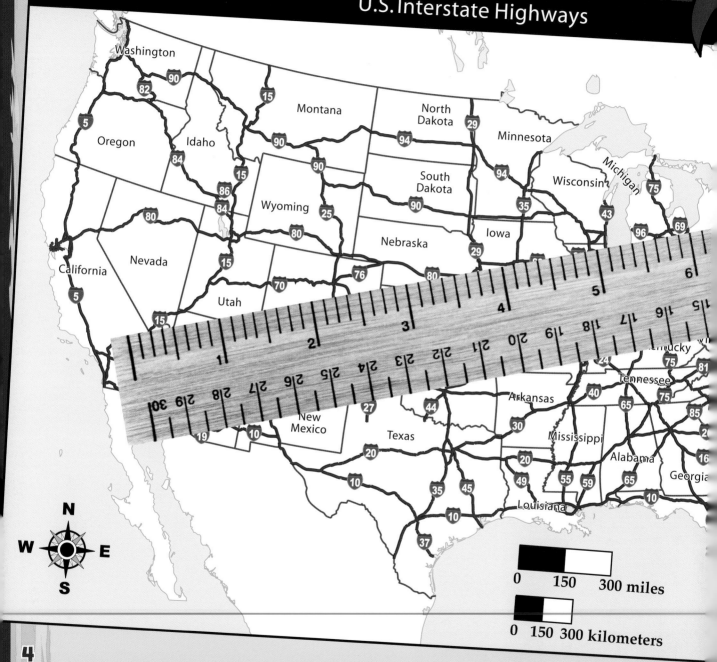

Washington

Oregon

Idaho

Montana

North Dakota

Minnesota

Michigan

California

Nevada

Utah

Wyoming

South Dakota

Wisconsin

Nebraska

Iowa

New Mexico

Texas

Arkansas

Tennessee

Kentucky

Mississippi

Alabama

Georgia

Louisiana

N
W E
S

0   150   300 miles

0   150   300 kilometers

My Map Shrunk the World!

I travel a lot. (Well, I am a bird.) When I need to know how far it is from here to there, I pull out my map.

But everything on my map is much smaller than in real life. It can't really be 5 inches from California to Wisconsin, can it?

Key

🛣 40	interstate highway
—	state border

No, the **distance** is much farther. Mapmakers take areas in the real world and draw them small enough to fit on paper.

But mapmakers put a code on each map. This code is called a **scale**. The scale **compares** distances on the earth to distances on the map. Come on! I'll show you how it works.

distance—the space between one place and another

scale—the label on a map that tells you what the map distance equals on the earth

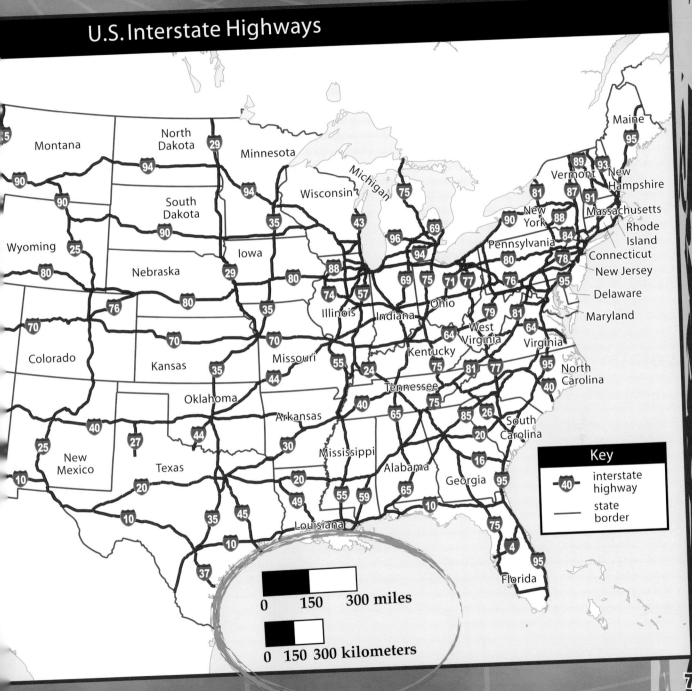

U.S. Interstate Highways

Key

interstate highway

state border

0   150   300 miles

0   150 300 kilometers

The Scale Tale

Different maps show different amounts of land. Small scale maps, like the map of North America, show big areas. It's called small because a small distance on the map equals a big distance on the earth.

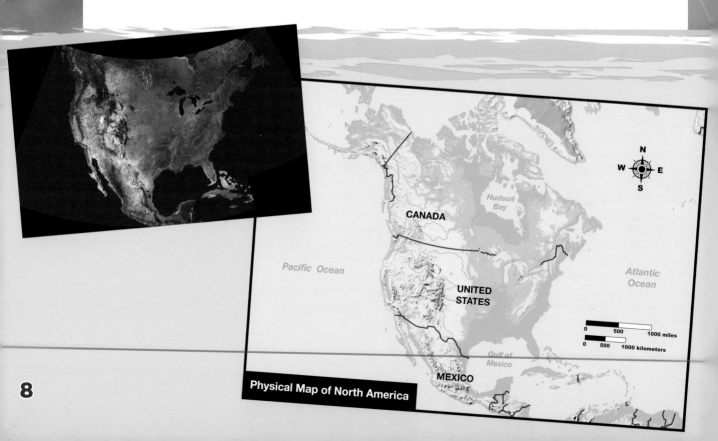

Physical Map of North America

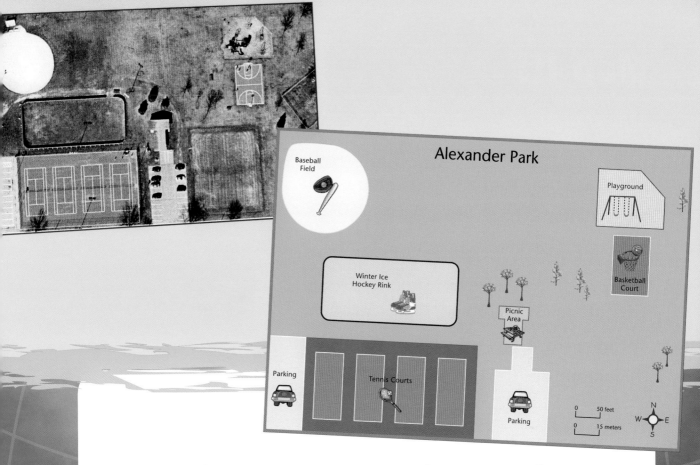

The opposite is true for maps that show smaller areas. Large scale maps, like the park map, show a small area of earth. The cool thing about these maps is that they show a lot of detail.

Map It!

Maps online are really cool. You can zoom in to see more detail. But did you know that the scale changes as you zoom? Look at these maps. One has a scale of 1 inch equals 1 mile. The other has a scale of 1 inch equals 1,000 feet. Can you see how the different scales affect the amount of detail you see?

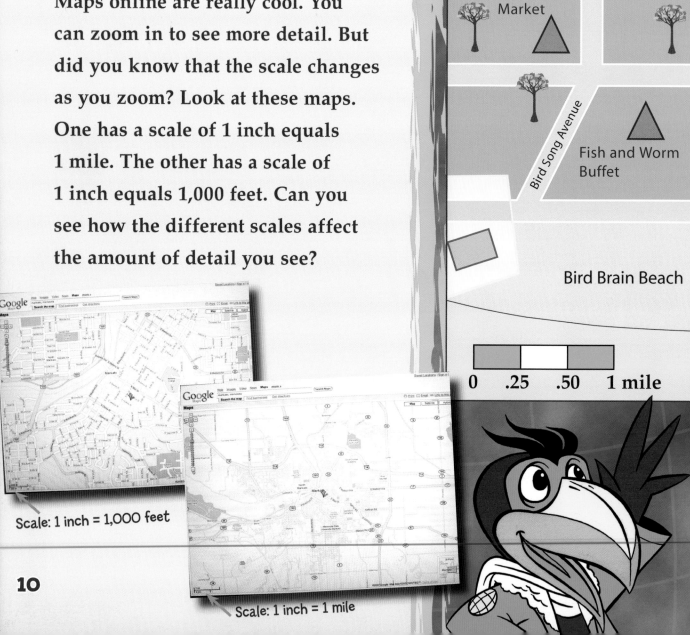

Loonville
"We're a little loony here"

Loonville Market

Bird Song Avenue

Fish and Worm Buffet

Bird Brain Beach

0   .25   .50   1 mile

Scale: 1 inch = 1,000 feet

Scale: 1 inch = 1 mile

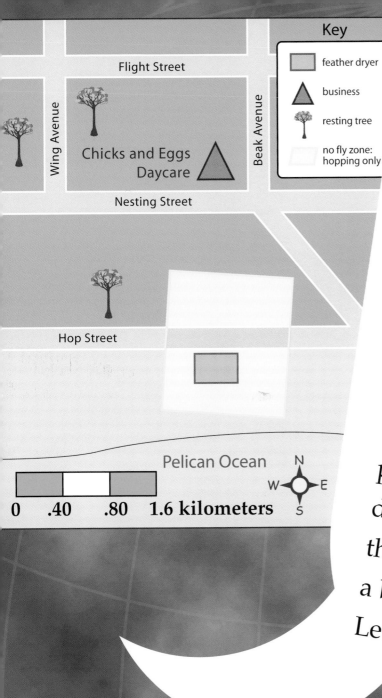

Key

feather dryer

business

resting tree

no fly zone:
hopping only

Flight Street

Wing Avenue

Beak Avenue

Chicks and Eggs
Daycare

Nesting Street

Hop Street

Pelican Ocean

N
W——E
S

0   .40   .80   1.6 kilometers

Use the Bar to Find How Far

One way to show scale is with a bar. Bar scales are divided into parts. Each part stands for a certain distance on the map. The number under each part tells you what distance that equals in the real world. Using a bar scale is simple. Let's try.

Let's see how far it is from Rocky Mountain National Park to Colorado Springs. First, use a ruler to measure the distance between the two points. Three inches. Now hold the ruler to the scale to see how many miles the inches **represent**. It's 100 miles.

Dinosaur
National
Monument

UTAH

Colorado River

Colorado
National
Monument

Grand
Junction

Mesa Verde
National Park

represent—to stand for something else

COLORADO

WYOMING

NEBRASKA

o Fort Collins

Rocky Mountain
National Park

KANSAS

⊗ Denver

0	25	50	75	100 miles

0	25	50	75	100 kilometers

Colorado
Springs

o Pueblo

KEY

⊗ capital

o city

~ river

points of
interest

national
forest

ROCKY MOUNTAINS

Great
Nati

Go Ratio!

Another kind of scale is shown by a **ratio**. This scale might look like 1:1,650. Ratio scales work for any **unit of measure**. But both numbers must stand for the same unit.

ratio—two numbers compared to each other

unit of measure—an inch, a centimeter, or any other amount that you use to find the size of something

Let's use inches. The first number, then, means 1 inch on the map. The second number means 1,650 actual inches. That means 1 map inch equals 1,650 earth inches.

Byward

Tower Hill

Tower Hill

Lower Thames Street

Tower of London

Saint Katherine's Way

Tower Bridge Approach

Thames River

N
W · E
S

Tower Bridge

Tower of London

Key

buildings

grassy areas

trees

water

roads

Scale
1:1,650

Scale
1:100

My Yard

Key

sandbox
swingset
tree
birdhouse

16

Let's use this map's ratio scale to find the distance from my house to the sandbox. First, measure the map distance. About two inches. Now, just count the inches by 100s. One inch equals 100 inches. Two inches equals 200 inches. That makes the sandbox 200 inches from my house.

X Marks the Fun Scales

Some maps use fun scales. A treasure map might use paces. Each pace could equal five footsteps on the ground. These scales aren't very exact, though. Your footsteps are bigger than my hops!

Scales can help you find how far on any map. Happy traveling!

One — equals five steps

Map It!

You can make weird scales. How many shoes would it take to reach across your bedroom? First, measure your shoe in inches. The scale would be one shoe equals that many inches. Now measure your room. How many shoes would it take to reach across your room? If you used a clown's shoe, would the scale be different?

Scales aren't only used on maps. When Mount Rushmore was planned, a model was made first. Each inch on the model stood for 1 foot on the cliff. To make the sculpture, workers measured the model in inches. Then they used the scale to figure out how many feet to cut away on the mountain.

Hands On: Looking for You

Here's a way for you and your friends to spice up hide-and-seek in your backyard.

What You Need

piece of paper
markers or colored pencils
ruler
paper rectangles

What You Do

1. Determine a scale for your map. Try 1 inch on the map equals 5 steps.
2. Walk the distance of your backyard, counting your steps.
3. On the paper, use the markers to draw an outline of your backyard. If it took 40 steps to walk one side of your yard, use the ruler to draw that side on the map 8 inches long.
4. Now pick out some features like trees or buildings. Walk the distance between these features and count your steps.
5. Draw the features on your map. Use the measurements you took and your scale to figure out where you need to put them.
6. Pick a good place to hide. Write some clues on the rectangles that lead your friends to the hiding spot. One clue might be: On the map, your first stop is 4 inches from the house. See if they can use your map and scale to find where you're hiding.

Glossary

compare (kuhm-PAIR)—to judge one thing against another

distance (DISS-tuhnss)—the amount of space between two places

ratio (RAY-shee-oh)—two numbers that are compared to each other

represent (rep-ri-ZENT)—to stand for something

scale (SKALE)—a label on the map that compares the distances on a map and the actual distances on earth

unit of measure (YOO-nit UHV MEZH-ur)—an amount that is used to find the size of something; an inch is a unit of measure.

Read More

Ashley, Susan. *I Can Read a Map.* I Can Do It! Milwaukee: Weekly Reader Early Learning Library, 2005.

Chancellor, Deborah. *Maps and Mapping.* Kingfisher Young Knowledge. New York: Kingfisher, 2004.

Wade, Mary Dodson. *Map Scale.* Rookie Read-About Geography. New York: Children's Press, 2003.

Internet Sites

FactHound offers a safe, fun way to find Internet sites related to this book. All of the sites on FactHound have been researched by our staff.

Here's how:
1. Visit *www.facthound.com*
2. Choose your grade level.
3. Type in this book ID **1429600535** for age-appropriate sites. You may also browse subjects by clicking on letters, or by clicking on pictures and words.
4. Click on the **Fetch It** button.

Facthound will fetch the best sites for you!

Index